Live with purpose!

Natalee
Knightli

Beautifully
Different

Beautifully Different

Living a Grand Slam Life Despite My Disability

Natalee Righetti

Foreword by Dave Righetti
San Francisco Giants Pitching Coach

ISBN:978-1470136512
Copyright © 2012 by Natalee Righetti

To contact Natalee Righetti,
email her at nataleerighetti@gmail.com

Cover Photograph:
Wesley Righetti

Designed and produced by
A Book in the Hand
San Francisco, California

*This book is dedicated to all my
family and friends who have supported
me through the many challenges I've faced,
as well as my successes. I know I wouldn't
be as driven to overcome all the obstacles
without your words of encouragement.*

—NJR

FOREWORD

On July 18, 1991, I was playing with the San Francisco Giants, and we were scheduled for a game in Montreal. I was flying with trepidation, knowing that back in Long Beach, California, my babies were pressing their way into the world. Sure enough, at about 4 p.m., I received a call from Kandice telling me that the triplets had arrived. Adrenaline surged through my body, and I didn't know what to do. My guilt was at an all-time high as I boarded the 5 p.m. bus to the stadium, since I had just missed their birth and still had a game to play that night. During the ride, I decided I needed to tell my manager Roger Craig the news, and then ask for a meeting after batting practice to tell the team.

Sitting in the locker room I went over what I might say. After all, my wife hadn't been pregnant, and nobody knew about the babies. I walked into Roger's office to tell him my story. I explained my guilt about missing the birth of my newborn triplets and that I didn't know what to do about that night's game. We decided it was best for me to catch an early flight in the morning because of the plane changes to get into Long Beach. With that decided, I finished dressing and thought about what to say to the team.

Batting practice went quickly that night. Afterwards, I walked into the locker room and got the team's attention. I wanted them to know about my situation—that I was the father and Kandice was the biological mother—and figured that most of them probably knew nothing about *in vitro* fertilization, the procedure we'd used to have our babies.

Starting my announcement, I was very nervous and tearing up. I let them know we had triplets and what the procedure was. As I was talking, my fellow teammate and pitcher, Don Robinson, asked me if I slept with my wife's sister Kayla, who had carried the babies. With everybody laughing, I told them that wasn't how it worked. By the time I finished, the guys were tearing up and congratulating me on the birth.

Now the tough part: I had a game later and might have to pitch. Sure enough, we ended up leading late in the game and I had to go in and close. I don't remember all the details, but I did save the game and we won a close one. I was anxious to get back to the hotel to call Kandice and let her know about the game and find out more about the kids.

Early the next morning, I went to the Montreal airport, forgetting that I didn't have a visa. When flying with the team, I don't need one and only need to fill out a declaration card. As my turn came with the French-speaking immigration agent, I told him I didn't have any papers other than my airline ticket. The agent didn't want to hear my story. Luckily, a nearby gentleman recognized me from my Yankee days and told the agent about my story in fluent French, and the agent let me through. I thanked him and my impromptu translator, signing autographs before gratefully boarding my flight.

After a couple of plane changes, I landed in Long Beach in the early evening and went straight to Long Beach Memorial Medical Center, anxious to see Kandice. When I arrived and made my way to the NICU, I was in a fog looking for her. Once I found her, we had a long hug, then a doctor walked up and told me about the birth and mentioned that Natalee had some sort of brain trauma. I didn't have any idea what he was saying. He handed me a pamphlet on brain trauma. I grabbed it, and then Kandice and I went into see the babies.

I didn't know what to expect but couldn't believe my eyes when I saw the three little ones in their incubators. They were so small! And purple. They couldn't have been any bigger than one of my hands. My memories of the rest of the day are vague, but I do remember Kandice and me going into the hospital chapel and doing some serious praying.

Despite the seriousness of the situation, I had a solid conviction that night and the next day that the babies would be just fine. I also knew that we would do everything we could to take care of them. Believe it or not, I had to fly back to Houston the next day to meet the team, knowing our lives were going to be very different.

Thinking back on that day now, it still astounds me how far Natalee has come and what a fighter she is. Saying I'm proud of her doesn't seem enough somehow, and yet that is the word that comes to mind. To have a daughter with a disability who still has a smile on her face every day and who now wants to help others feel good about themselves is a rare gift I will always treasure. I hope in reading her book, you get a glimpse into what is possible when you have a life that is beautifully different.

~ *Dave Righetti*

A NOTE FROM THE AUTHOR

For a long time, I've known that I would write a motivational book about having a disability. I pictured it happening after I was married and had children, writing about the challenges of being a wife and mother who has to navigate daily life with the use of only one hand. Recently though, I started writing down my stories of living with a disability and realized I already had a lot to share.

Even as a little girl, I knew there was something different about me, but I never felt being born with cerebral palsy and the lack of ability that came with it was a bad thing. I've come to learn that if I want something badly enough and work hard enough to get it, I can achieve anything despite the challenges I face. This work ethic paid off with my writing and as my stories multiplied, I ended up finishing this book just two months shy of turning twenty.

My hope is that this book not only inspires others with disabilities, but anyone who faces challenges of any kind. My purpose in writing it is to show others the positive things that can come from embracing what makes you different. To me, my disability is both an ability and a tool I can use to my advantage. Right now, I'm using it to inspire others to make the best of the life they've been given. Someday, it will be a large part of what makes a strong and lasting partnership with my future someone and later what will make my children empathetic, humble, and independent human beings. There is nothing in my life that I wish was different because I've been given a gift, and I want to help others discover their gifts too.

~ *Natalee Righetti*

TABLE OF CONTENTS

Blessings

Circumstance

Acceptance

Purpose

Destiny

Blessings

Count your blessings,

for they will make

you grateful for the

life you have.

CHAPTER 1

It Started with a Love Story

It was love at first sight that night in 1988. From the moment they met, and got to talking and laughing, they realized they did not want to be without each other. Six short months later, they got married.

At least that is how I always imagine my mom and dad's love story. A real-life fairytale. My dad, tall, dark-haired, tan, and athletic, and my mom, brunette, bright-eyed, and slim-figured, really are perfect for each other. Every time I hear the story of how their life together started, I cannot help but wonder if my love story will be anything like theirs. My mom tells their story perfectly.

When I was fifteen, I found out I would
never be able to carry a child. That knowledge
forced me to think more about getting married
one day than maybe I otherwise would have. I
got a little obsessed with the idea that no man
would ever want me, and thought I'd better
figure out a way to make my situation not so
bad. While in college, I had to write a research
paper on a topic of my choice. I looked into
surrogacy. It was a fairly unheard of thing back
in the late 80s, but I thought it gave me some
hope. Once I knew that surrogacy was a possibility, I felt a little less pathetic.

I dated a lot and learned through those
experiences just what I was looking for in
the perfect guy. Not that I was perfect. But I
certainly wasn't going to settle. The month I
turned twenty-four, I went with a girlfriend to
our usual Bay Area hot spot to dance. I had been
there many times, but this night was different.
Little did I know it would be my last time going
there, since there really was no need after what
happened that night.

Reluctantly, I went to Pepper's with a friend who had recently broken up with her boyfriend, and she really needed to get out and have some fun. We arrived unusually early that night and the club hadn't even opened yet, so we killed time in the bar area as we waited. A tall, good-looking guy in a white-and-gray striped dress shirt walked past me and caught my eye. I wasn't there looking for anyone, and in fact, it had only been about a month since I stopped seeing someone.

Evidently, my friend's father collected baseball cards and had several photos in his office, and she recognized one of the other guys in the group from those photos. She went to talk to him. I stayed away but she soon pulled me in and introduced me. The only guy I cared to talk to was that guy in the striped shirt. We connected instantly. He asked me my name and when I said "Kandice Owen," he said, "Owens?" I said, "No 's' but my grandma was Owens, and dropped the 's' when she married my grandpa Owen." His grandma Reghetto had married his

grandpa Righetti. Weird! Funny similarity, we thought, and an icebreaker for sure.

We danced all night, getting pretty flirty. His friends were shocked to see that he was dancing at all, since he never did. Of course, they were slow dances, so it was mostly just holding and swaying. We continued talking in the bar area until the club closed. I thought, "How nice. Too bad I'll never see him again."

My friend slept over at my house that night (I still lived at home with my mom and dad). In the morning, the phone rang and she answered it. She handed it to me with a look of disbelief and whispered, "You're going to marry this guy!"

I said, "Yeah, right!"

We walked into the kitchen where my parents had breakfast ready. My friend told them about the guy we met and blurted out that she thought I'd end up marrying him. I laughed it off, but didn't deny the idea at all. Then my dad told us of this premonition he had. He was

watching a baseball game a couple nights before, and noticed that the pitcher had a strong presence about him. He remembered thinking, *I sure wish my daughter would meet a confident guy like that.* I think my dad was tired of seeing me go out with guys who were not "good enough" for me, or seeing me get hurt by guys who were wrong for me. Of course, you don't know any of this until you meet THE guy. And Dave was just that. THE guy. My Mr. Right. Only, I didn't know it yet.

I found out quickly that it's tough to meet a guy you like a lot, but can't even see again until his season ends, which in baseball is usually October. Dave was pitching for the Yankees, so after meeting him in August, I didn't get to see him again until he got back to the Bay Area in mid-October. However, we talked on the phone every day after the day we met, and we would talk forever. Some nights he would fall asleep on the other end because he was exhausted, but neither of us wanted to hang up. One time his phone bill was $700! I even timed my night

class at Cal State-Fullerton to be home by
10:30 p.m. for his call. One night, I got pulled
over for speeding. I thought the female police
officer would understand my dilemma, but no
such luck.

We fell in love over the phone. Sure, we
were both struck by Cupid's arrow the night we
met, but it was the phone calls that clinched it.
In fact, we could not remember what the other
looked like, so we exchanged photos. He sent
me some baseball photos and magazine articles
about him, which was a great way for me to
learn more about him. I dug out my old model-
ing photos, which I wasn't sure still even looked
like me, but they were the best I could find.

When he finally got home from his
season, he asked if he could court me. My answer was a definite "yes," so we were ready for
our official first date. I went to pick him up at
the airport, it was under heavy construction so
the gates were temporarily moved. I wasn't experienced with airports anyway, and with all the

construction confusion and not having seen him in months, we nearly missed each other!

I don't think he actually met my family until the next visit though. At the end of his first visit, I took him to the airport and we sat in a café waiting for his flight. He said he wanted to come back in a week, and that he would drive this time. It struck me that things were getting serious. I knew I had to tell him that I couldn't keep seeing him, knowing he was falling for me as much as I was for him and he still didn't know my secret.

I told him there was something I needed to tell him. "It's only fair that you know that I can never carry a child." He looked at me a bit surprised, not because of what I had told him, but because I actually thought that could change his mind about me. He said, "If I were to marry you, it would be because I want to spend the rest of my life with you. Not because you could give me children." Wow! My heart raced. I knew then that he was sent to me from God.

Blessings

Six months later, we were married. I truly believe there is a right person out there for each of us. If you're lucky enough to find that right person, together, you can get through any challenge life throws your way. Dave and I didn't know it at the time, but we were to face many challenges when it was time for us to expand our family.

CHAPTER 2

Generosity

During spring training of 1990—my dad's first year with the San Francisco Giants—my parents found a surrogate mother and were excited to expand their family. A surrogate either has another woman's fertilized egg surgically implanted or is artificially inseminated, and then carries the child for the other woman until birth, usually for a fee. However, my parents excitement was short lived because at the last minute, the surrogate backed out.

My mom had planned a trip to Southern California to visit her sister Kayla and see her three-month-old niece Mallory for the first time. My mom was also

supposed to meet her surrogate, who would be flying in from Minnesota, but unfortunately had to bring the devastating news to her sister instead. Even though the two sisters had anxiously awaited this first meeting with Mallory, the mood quickly changed when my mom arrived. Kayla could tell that she was happy to be there but was also holding back tears. My mom told Kayla and her husband Mark that her surrogate had backed out.

As they sat in the backyard that afternoon, Kayla told my mom she would love to help her, but didn't want to assume her husband would be okay with something so life altering. My mom never asked Kayla to carry her child, but my aunt could see that gleam of hope in my mom's eyes as they imagined that possibility together.

Kayla could not stop thinking about how badly she wanted to help her sister. Her heart knew that her purpose was to carry a child for my mom, but she had no idea how to bring up the subject with Mark. That evening, Mark called Kayla from work and said he wanted to discuss something with her when he got home. "It's about your sister," he said. Kayla prayed she

would get the answer she longed to hear. As it turned out, my uncle wanted to help my mom and dad just as much as my aunt did. He told Kayla that he would fully support her if she chose to be my mom's surrogate. My aunt told my mom the great news over the phone. Mom got Dad's approval, who was also thrilled.

Both my mom's sisters, Kayla and Kim, and her brother Jim's wife Dawn, all offered to carry a baby for my parents, but it was a better time in Kayla's life to do it. After talking to Mark, Kayla made it official and that special moment is one my parents, and my aunt and uncle cherish to this day. My parents' prayers were answered, but it was just the beginning of a long journey for both couples.

Shortly after the decision was made, Kayla began a series of ultrasounds and blood tests to prepare. My mom and dad had already begun the process of fertilization and had eighteen frozen embryos waiting to be thawed and implanted. However, my mom's embryos could not be implanted into Kayla yet, because her system was not completely back to normal after giving birth to Mallory and breastfeeding for three months.

By August 1990, the embryo transfer was complete. The procedure Kayla went through was simple, with hardly any pain, but that was the easy part. She would soon realize the long road ahead of her would not be as painless. Kayla had to be given daily progesterone injections along with five days of bed rest. During this time, she got a lot of help from her family. After a slow two weeks, Kayla thought she could be pregnant. She took a pregnancy test right away, but it came back negative. She did not understand how that could be, since she did everything the doctors asked of her.

They tried another embryo transfer on October 18. This time, Mom stayed in town for a few days to help her sister. Kayla's injections were more painful this time, and it hurt to move her legs or lay on her side. Another two weeks went by after yet another transfer, and another pregnancy test was done. After several ultrasounds, the test came back negative again.

Distraught, Kayla called my mom and dad. She tried her best to hide her crying. It was a very emotional time. She didn't know if the tears were

because she wasn't pregnant or because she knew she had to keep getting more tests and ultrasounds. Having doctors look at her under a microscope, so to speak, did not make Kayla feel like the most glamorous person, and in fact, was quite humiliating at times with up to three doctors in the room at any given time.

Still, my aunt and my parents chose to give it a try for a third time after Christmas, so nothing would conflict with the holidays. Out of frozen embryos, my mom began a series of injections to make her ovaries produce multiple eggs, while my aunt took injections to prepare her body for pregnancy. Their cycles needed to be synchronized so my aunt's uterine lining would be ready for the transfer two days after fertilization of my mom's eggs. My mom had 30-something eggs extracted, which caused her immense pain. She could not even sit upright or move for quite a while due to her stomach being so tender. Kayla lovingly told my mom, "Don't ever let anyone tell you that you never experienced the pain that comes with childbirth."

CHAPTER 3

Miracles

At the end of January 1991, five or six embryos were implanted in my aunt. One week later, on February 5, when Kayla was going through human chorionic gonadotropin injections to keep her uterine lining favorable for pregnancy, she had her first bout with morning sickness while getting out of her car at the grocery store. Physically, she felt horrible, but she was excited too because this time, she had a good feeling. When my aunt got home from the store, she received a call from her doctor.

Doctor: *We have your pregnancy test back, and this time it is good news.*

Kayla: *Oh, I knew it!*

Doctor: *I have some concerns though.*

Kayla: *What kind of concerns?*

Doctor: *I think there is more than one baby.*

Kayla: *Twins! That is perfect.*

Doctor: *Well, a normal pregnancy test value is about one hundred, and yours is almost 700.*

Kayla: *What does that mean?*

Doctor: *Are you sitting down?*

Kayla: *Yes.*

Doctor: *It's a multiple pregnancy. I think maybe three or four!*

At the first ultrasound on February 14, the doctors could see three embryos, but could not detect any heartbeats yet. Kayla sent my mom pictures of the ultrasounds.

On February 20, Kayla had one of the scariest days of her pregnancy. She started bleeding and had a little bit of cramping, which were complications she was familiar with from her previous pregnancy. All Kayla could think about was my mom and how she absolutely could not lose this pregnancy. She called the

doctor right away, and he told her to come in for an ultrasound. Through the ultrasound, the doctor could see a blood-filled sac. He told my aunt that there had been a miscarriage, and one did not make it, but he continued to check the other sacs that still had a heart beat. The doctor showed Kayla the screen to reassure her. "There's one… there's one… and wait, wait, look at this… there's another! There must have been four!"

Although she was sad that one baby had not survived, my aunt was not so sure she could have handled carrying quadruplets. Early in her pregnancy, Kayla was able to run short errands and could watch her son Cory's league games from a lounge chair in the outfield. However, she had to stop working as a nurse after a few months, so my parents chipped in to make sure the pregnancy did not affect her family financially.

My aunt, as well as the rest of her family, sacrificed a lot to give my parents children. During Kayla's pregnancy, five-year-old Cory came down with the chicken pox and sixteen-month-old Mallory caught them soon after. Days later, Kayla experienced

preterm labor and was admitted to a nearby hospital, then transferred to Long Beach Memorial Medical Center.

My contagious cousins were not allowed to see their mother for about a week and a half. From her hospital bed, Aunt Kayla felt helpless. One of the tough things about not being able to see her kids as much as she wanted was that she was missing out on key moments in their lives. At one point, Mallory started calling her grandma "mom."

Just when it all seemed to get too tough to handle, little things would happen to remind her that what she was doing was worth it. She would be lying in bed and could feel one of the babies wake up, and soon all three of us were "dancing" in her tummy. Aunt Kayla could not help but laugh in disbelief that she was carrying triplets.

My mom, of course, wanted to be there every step of the way, but my aunt encouraged her to go on road trips with my dad. It would be the last time they could spend this much time together for many years. Mom

also wanted to get the house prepared before her life became consumed by three newborns.

Being around her sister was reassuring for my mom, and she did everything she could to keep Kayla at ease. Whatever Kayla needed help with, my mom filled in. One time, after being in Southern California for a few weeks, it was time for my mom to go home. Her maternal instincts must have kicked in because she was hesitant to leave. The same night my mom left, my aunt went into preterm labor after just twenty-seven weeks of pregnancy.

When Mark got home from work, Kayla was lying on the couch having contractions. He drove his wife to the hospital, where she was immediately put on medication to help stop the contractions. This time, Kayla's cervix had dilated about one to two centimeters.

The doctors thought they had the contractions under control, so they sent Mark home and let my mom know she did not need to worry about flying back down. Aunt Kayla was able to sleep for a while. She awoke with severe cramping and started having

contractions every ten to fifteen minutes. When the nurse checked on her, she said her contractions were nothing to worry about because they were fifteen minutes apart and were mild. By the time the nurse came in a second time, Kayla was having more cramping, and the contractions were even stronger.

When the doctor came in, he said the babies were ready to make their entrance so they decided to get Kayla to the operating room. Although Aunt Kayla expected something like this to happen, she did not think it would be so dramatic. She started to hyperventilate as questions and worried thoughts bounced around her head.

The doctor explained that he was going to put a mask over her mouth, and that they were about to do a Caesarean section to deliver the babies faster. Kayla could feel herself fighting the anesthesia. A nurse poked her head in the door and said, "Kayla, your parents are here!" After that, she was able to relax, knowing someone who loved her was there. She took a deep breath and said, "Let's go!"

CHAPTER 4

Obstacles

My brother, sister, and I came into the world sooner than expected. Our original due date was in October, but we decided July 19 was our day. Nineteen has always been a lucky number in our family. On July 19, 1990, exactly a year before we were born, my dad passed Hall of Famer Whitey Ford by setting a record for the most appearances in Yankee franchise history (499). It was also Dad's jersey number with both the Yankees and the Giants. And even though it's also the day my grandpa Leo Righetti (a Minor League Baseball player in the

early 1950s) died, the number 19 is significant in our family and makes us believe it is our magic number.

Nicolette Kay was born first, then Wesley David followed a minute later. And then two minutes after him, I, Natalee Jean, entered the world. There we laid in incubators, hooked up to breathing tubes. We had each suffered varying degrees of complications due to our early arrival and lack of oxygen during the Caesarean section. The odds were against us, but we would prove that we were not going to give up without a fight.

My aunt and other family members visited us in the hospital each day. My dad, on the other hand, was in Montreal playing the Expos on the day we were born and had to pitch that same night. Arriving at the hospital a day later, he was not prepared for the sight of his three little ones needing so much medical intervention.

Weighing just two pounds each, Nicolette, Wesley, and I spent two months in the hospital. My mom could fit her wedding ring around four of my

fingers. Our family watched us go from requiring breathing tubes to relying less and less on oxygen, and from being fed through a tube to finally drinking from a bottle. Yet because of our low birth weight and under-developed lungs filled with fluid, my family was well aware of the possibility that we would not make it. With each passing day, the seriousness of each of our medical conditions became more apparent.

Wesley suffered the least damage from birth — the grade one bleed in his brain healed on its own. Nicolette was diagnosed with a yeast infection in her blood stream, and my parents' only option was to give her a medication that could zap her hearing. They felt their child not being able to hear was a smaller price to pay considering that her life was at risk. My mom once told me that I was a miracle baby, since my medical complications ended up being more severe than my brother's and sister's.

Being born last meant I was in the back of my aunt's uterus and received less oxygen than my siblings. Because of this, I suffered a mild stroke that caused two bleeds in my brain. The third-degree bleed on the left

side healed on its own, but the fourth-degree one on the right—the most severe type—caused major brain damage. My hydrocephalus, a buildup of fluid inside the skull, led to brain swelling. A neurosurgeon inserted a ventriculoperitoneal shunt on the right side of my head to drain the cerebral fluid, relieve pressure, and avoid more fluid buildup.

After two months in the NICU, my parents could finally take us home. The doctors came close to keeping me in the hospital a little while longer, but decided at the last minute that I could go home too. My mom's words help me understand the depth of my parents' love and strength during this difficult time.

> *My kids were meant to be in this world, and had Dave and I not found each other, that would not have been possible. We have been blessed in so many ways through finding each other, my sister offering to be our surrogate, the fact that they all pulled through after an early entry into this world, that they are doing so well despite some major obstacles, and the love that*

both sides of our families have given us all. I know that each of my kids has someone out there who is just right for them. They may not know it now, but they will know when it happens.

❧

Circumstance

Trust your heart, and

life will lead you where

you are meant to be.

CHAPTER 5

The Diagnosis

When my dad arrived at the hospital in Long Beach, the first thing the doctor gave him was a book about cerebral palsy, a form of paralysis believed to be caused by a prenatal brain defect or an injury to the brain during birth. I was diagnosed with hemiplegic cerebral palsy, which means I have less control of the muscles on the left half of my body. My brain can't send different signals to both sides of my body at the same time, so if I want to move my left hand a certain way, my right hand has to do the same motion.

I practiced over and over again in physical and occupational therapy, moving my left foot, leg, hand, and arm while trying not to move anything on the right side of my body. It was emotionally and physically draining to focus so hard on things like moving just one finger on my left hand. The first seventeen years of my life were spent going to physical therapy for my lower extremities and occupational therapy for my upper extremities.

My parents were aware that I could also develop epilepsy and would see that prediction come true: When I was two, I had my first and most severe seizure. Our live-in nanny found me in my crib, frothing at my mouth. My mom called 911, and an ambulance came right away. The doctors did everything they could, but weren't able to snap me out of it.

That seizure lasted two hours, and I was hospitalized and given high doses of adult seizure medication that left me lethargic. My mom worried that I would never be the same, especially after the doctors said, "We don't know for sure." After I came home from the hospital, I had a seizure every six months until I was three.

Eventually, the seizures grew further apart, and I remember keeping track so I would know when to expect the next one. As I got older, they came about every three years. Every night as I got into bed, even though I was on medication, I hoped I would not wake up with the feeling of an oncoming seizure. Although the fear and dread was horrible, it was the time before and after my seizures that I hated the most.

On the mornings I had seizures, I would wake up dizzy, shaky, and short of breath. As my heart raced, panic would set in as I realized another seizure was about to start. I would then fall unconscious, unaware of my surroundings, and go into seizure mode. Usually, I would wake up on the ground weakened and tired.

I was the only one in my family who woke up with the birds at six. There were times I would have a seizure and my parents were not around to help, since I almost always had them right after I woke up. Luckily, I haven't had a seizure for seven years, but my last one still haunts me.

On August 12, 2004, I woke up and went down-

stairs. My mom and dad were talking in the kitchen before my dad had to leave for work. As I went to give my mom a hug, I tried to tell her I felt dizzy, but fell to the ground before I could get the words out. My mom tried her best to keep me from falling too hard, and my dad rushed to get a pillow to put under my head for support. Wesley put a wet rag under my neck. They were used to this drill.

For ten minutes, they yelled my name and patted my cheeks with their hands to get me to gain consciousness quicker. My mom told my dad in a worried panic, "Don't hit her cheeks too hard!" But thanks to my dad, I gradually became more conscious.

I tried to get up as soon as I came to. My parents told me to slow down, but I was not about to let that monster of a seizure make me feel powerless. Feeling tired and limp, I made my way to the couch. As soon as my dad was sure I was okay, he left for the ballpark.

To cheer me up, the rest of my family stayed in the living room with me and watched *Lara Croft: Tomb Raider* on TV. I was happy that my family wanted to

make me feel better, but I sat there feeling foolish and inferior about what had just happened. It had been two years since my last seizure, and just when I felt like I didn't need to be scared anymore, another seizure surprised me.

After being seizure-free for seven years, I am now not as fearful about waking with an aura of shakiness. However, I still make sure to count my blessings and pray I do not have another one in my lifetime. Not having total control over what happens to my body and when is so unsettling. Living with cerebral palsy and epilepsy is often frustrating, and I grew tired of doctors and physical therapists having so much control over my life. I stubbornly learned the hard way that they were just trying to help.

CHAPTER 6

Physical Therapy

Years after I went to her the first time when I was two years old, one of my first physical therapists told me that I was a little ball of energy running around the room. I really enjoyed going to physical therapy until I was about six, because I got to do fun activities. Then I changed physical and occupational therapists and was forced to do things I did not want to do. Going to therapy was not fun anymore. In fact, I dreaded it.

I most feared the appointments when my physical therapist would evaluate my progress. Despite

the fact I am highly active for someone with cerebral palsy, those meetings usually ended with my mom setting up an appointment for me to get casted to stretch my left ankle. At night, I had to wear a leg brace to stretch my ankle. Not only did it hurt, but the brace was so uncomfortable that I had a hard time sleeping. I told my therapist, but he just assumed I was making up excuses.

At this point in my life, I felt I was being punished for having a disability because of having to go through all the physical therapy and evaluations. Wasn't it enough just to live with a disability? It seemed that I left that place in tears every time. How could people I did not know very well have so much control over my life? There were many things I feared facing in therapy, but I learned to overcome them by believing in myself and wanting to do better.

All those years taught me to push what scared me to the back of my mind so I could conquer it. One of my biggest fears, even today, is walking down a flight of stairs. Stepping down onto another step with my left foot was hard for me to learn because my body was off balance, and I did not have the same amount of feeling in my left foot as in my right. After practicing during several physical therapy sessions, I was able to walk down stairs with the assistance of a right-side railing. Not letting fear run my life drove me to overcome something I did not want to do, and it is what motivates me every time I face going down a flight of stairs.

My occupational therapists worked with me to do tasks with both hands as much as possible. I learned to tie my shoes and button my shirt and pants. Today, I try to use the skills I learned as a little girl, but some things are easier for me to do with one hand. Well, maybe not easier, but quicker, and I like to get things done as fast as I can. I carry out daily tasks like washing my hair, getting dressed, and typing on a computer with one hand.

As I got older and became interested in sports, therapy served a different purpose: to help me play sports. I wanted to take on that challenge not because athletes run in my family, but because sports are hard for someone with a physical disability to be successful

at. Therapy evolved from something that helped equip me for everyday life into something that would help me hold my own on a sports team. I practiced every motor skill exercise until I was mentally and physically drained. Every push-up I did, I gave it my all knowing that one day, if I worked hard enough, I could call myself an athlete.

CHAPTER 7

Dad, Baseball, and Life Lessons

I sat in awe of what was before me. At nine years old, the ballpark many know as the home of the San Francisco Giants seemed bigger than life to me. My siblings and I were born into the world of baseball; a world that we would get to know well for the next twenty-plus years of our lives. My days were filled with school and doctor's appointments, but on the weekends, I would get to go to Giants games. I've always loved watching the games and seeing my dad run out to the mound

to give the pitcher words of wisdom. I also loved the atmosphere of the stadium.

Baseball games have always been an escape for me, and AT&T Park became my home away from home. It's where I could forget about my medical problems, the pressure from school, and all the other stresses that anyone faces when they're growing up. Baseball games were where I felt the most alive: the stadium lights shining down on the field, the noise of the fans around me, and the smell of garlic fries are all part of my DNA. And every time I step into the ballpark, I know I am there to support my dad.

My dad travels eight months out of the year and staying involved in baseball has kept our family close, but it is not always an easy lifestyle.

When my dad is away on road trips, my mom, siblings, and I feel a definite absence in the house, but seeing him on TV helps us feel like we are there with him. Whenever we see him running out to the mound or talking to his pitchers in the dugout, we cheer him on as he gives advice that seems to really help his pitchers win games. Our family believes in sticking together and supporting my dad, as well as each other, in any way we can: watching Giants games on TV, going on occasional road trips, and attending as many home games as possible.

My dad doesn't always get to witness in person the events in our lives, but he doesn't miss out on much because he calls every morning and night to talk to my mom and then the rest of us.

My dad and I have had a special bond ever since I was born. I am the only one he gave a nickname to— little peanut. Despite the fact that I have not been able to see him as much as I would have liked growing up, our bond has remained strong, even as life keeps changing around us.

Our phone conversations have always been special to me. We started talking on the phone as soon as I was able to speak full sentences as a toddler. I told him anything and everything that came to mind. Throughout the years, our conversations were often about baseball. I watched all the games and kept up with

the players' stats. I watched baseball so I could stay connected with my dad.

As I got older, our conversations shifted from baseball to other topics, and one of our talks in particular really touched my heart. During spring training one year, we talked on the phone for a long time, longer than usual. I always knew my dad had confidence in me and was proud of me, but it didn't really sink in until he told me that he knew he would not need to worry about me being on my own one day or being a good wife, because he had confidence in how I handled myself. To my surprise, he told me that even though people have said I am just like him, *it is him who is just like me.* He said he was proud of that—proud to be like his daughter. I am proud to be like him as well. It was the best compliment anyone has ever given me, and I will never forget that phone call. It meant the world to me for him to say that.

There have been times when our conversations sounded more like arguments instead of light-hearted chats, which doesn't surprise me since we are both

strongly opinionated and hard headed. At times, I was unsure if having that same quality was a good thing, but I now think it has helped me excel in life. The truth is, I am proud of my stubbornness. Sometimes it resulted in bad decisions, but it also helped me be able to say, "I have a disability, and I am still capable of doing anything I dream of doing."

That night, I learned that my dad and I had more than just stubbornness in common. Underneath his strong, composed façade is a passionate, wise, and caring soul. To him, having a career is about giving respect as well as getting it, doing what he loves and what he's good at, and passionately teaching others the things that have helped him throughout his life. It has never been about success or money, though the money has certainly made it easier for him to take care of his family. Like him, I plan to have a career that I'm passionate about, and that allows me to teach others some of what I've learned.

My parents' strong devotion to each other despite all the time apart continues to amaze me. I am sure it is

hard being away from the one you love, so I try my best to be a companion for my mom while my dad is on the road. Mom shows so much support for what Dad does for a living, and I know he appreciates it and respects her for that.

When the San Francisco Giants won the World Series, my family had even more opportunities to be together. My mom, brother, sister, and I went to almost every playoff game, as well as every World Series game. These past twelve years have been quite a journey, filled with criticism from outsiders, and the stress of some seasons not going as well as we all hoped. Winning the World Series made it all worth it.

My favorite moment of the World Series was not at any of the games, but after the sixth and final game against the Texas Rangers. After that game, my mom, brother, sister, and I met up with my dad in the dining room of the visitors' clubhouse. Without saying a word, I reached out to Dad for a congratulatory hug as tears welled up in my eyes. My dad started to cry, along with the rest of my family, as we continued to hug each other.

The tears we cried during that special moment were not only tears of joy, but also tears of relief. My dad, along with the rest of the team, worked tirelessly for that World Series title. Tough season after tough season, they never gave up and finally got what they deserved. What many people do not realize is that professional athletes, and everyone involved in professional sports, are all just normal people trying to make a living so that they can provide for themselves and their families. It is unfortunate the amount of criticism they have to put up with, when they are trying the best they can to do their job. Baseball is not just a sport to these men and their families; it is how they make a living.

That is life though. Not everyone will sympathize with you or try to understand the choices you make, and that is one thing my dad, a former starter and closer, is familiar with. He has been in the baseball business for a very long time and has been through the ups and downs that baseball puts many players through. He empathizes with his pitchers and puts his heart and soul into making the pitching staff the best they can be.

My dad is a great coach, but he makes an even better husband and father. He is one of the most loyal, respectful, and loving men I know, and for that he will always have my love and support. I do not see Dad as just a professional athlete, I see him as someone whose respect, passion, and commitment to baseball allowed him to become so successful. I'm proud to be his daughter and will carry out the traits he has given me throughout my lifetime. The success he has had may be one of the reasons why I am looked at differently, but that is what my life is... beautifully different. I wouldn't have it any other way.

❧

Acceptance

Instead of being angry

about life not going the

way you want it to,

embrace the changes it

brings and learn from it.

CHAPTER 8

School Days

My life circumstances have helped me learn the difference between what is important to me and what is not. I have never been the type to stay out late, party, or get high on marijuana. Although I understand why kids want to experiment with those things, I have never felt it was for me. When I look back on high school, I do not regret not experimenting like the typical teenager, but instead think I did myself a favor because of the medical problems I have had to deal with.

While my peers were out having fun and being carefree, I was at home researching my disability so I

could improve the quality of my life. I've lived my entire life fearing something would go wrong with my body, and I didn't want to do anything that could possibly set me back. High school was when my seizures were finally under control, and I didn't want to fear them starting up again. I didn't know if drinking or getting high would cause a seizure or otherwise put my body at risk, and I wasn't willing to take the chance.

So rather than worry about the types of experiences that most teenagers seem so eager to have, I thought about how the decisions I made would affect my physical well-being and my future. Facing this reality and making decisions about my health forced me to mature faster than other kids in my grade. Because of that, and also being a year older than most people in my grade, I often felt like I didn't belong in high school.

My medical condition may have kept me from becoming a typical rebellious teenager, and I was okay with that. Part of me was still curious but there were just too many different things I had to think about. Because my life has always been a serious matter, I

never really went through the normal stage of thinking a relationship was more important than everything else. Having a boyfriend was never a priority, because I did not want to fall into the trap of needing to be desired by someone in order to feel good about myself. I wanted to make sure I knew what I wanted out of my life and the person I wanted to be, before I shared my heart with someone else.

During my junior high and high school years, I was still in the process of accepting myself as a disabled person, and it was important for me to accept who I was before I let anyone—guys mostly—get to know me on a personal level. A lot of the reason I was so closed off to guys was the fact that my dad was a public figure. I was afraid that guys only liked me because I was the daughter of a major league pitching coach and former pitcher. And in fact, there were a few times when I felt some people I went to school with—and maybe a boy or two—only wanted to get to know me because of my ties to the baseball world.

I tried my best not to let my insecurities show, in the hopes that my peers would see me as a normal

person and like me for me. Looking back, I sometimes used my fear of people liking me only for the baseball connection as an excuse to close myself off from others. My real fear was someone not liking me because of my disability.

Throughout my school years, I faced hurtful looks and words from others that naturally discouraged me. I lived through many experiences where kids were bothered by the way my hand and arm looked. One day, during engineering class in eighth grade, a boy yelled across the classroom, "Why does your arm look like that?" Here I was, one of the only girls in the class and the only one with a disability, just trying to do my work and build things. My teacher quickly shut down his remark and made sure to let me know afterward that my disability was hardly noticeable, but I was still embarrassed.

At school, my peers frequently judged me—whether it was about how badly the Giants were doing or about something being wrong with my body—and I always felt like I had to defend myself. Some people even acted disgusted by the way my disability made me

look. I never really thought of myself as someone to be freaked out by, and it wasn't until junior high that I found out what that felt like. Making fun of a person's disability is shameful. Whatever makes each person different is also what makes him or her interesting and unique. That is why I make it known to anybody who doubts me that my disability is also a rare ability.

I learned through experience that I didn't need to worry about why people wanted to be part of my life. Being comfortable in my own skin and confident in who I am as a person is what intrigues others and makes them want to get to know me. Kirsten Wessbecher, my best friend growing up, helped me realize that.

Kirsten and I have always shared the same values of staying true to ourselves and treating others with the kind of respect we wanted to receive. I always knew I could trust her and be myself around her. She accepted my disability without hesitation and made what caused me to feel so different seem so normal. Having her friendship on my side throughout elementary school and junior high was what helped get me through. I never was concerned about how many friends I had

because I had one true friend who cared about me for the person I was.

Other kids, however, were not always considerate about how I did things. They would point out my stiff left arm and how it was bent, as well as the way being double-jointed made my hand look. Things like that hurt my self-esteem and regretfully, I became a very defensive person for a while. I have always been feisty, the kind of girl who does not put up with other people's negative opinions about how I look or act. But those years in school made it tough not to snap at people who put me down.

I even had P.E. teachers who discouraged me, making me feel incapable of doing things. I will never forget putting 100 percent into a push-up test, only to have the teacher call me "weak."

At that time, I had been getting Botox treatments in my arm. People usually associate Botox with looking younger by reducing wrinkles. Actually, Botox, or botulinum toxin type A, is a muscle-soothing compound that has been used for people with cerebral palsy to

decrease stiffness and muscle spasms. Botox weakened the tense muscles in my arm that were always working so that I could learn to use the underdeveloped muscles. After my first treatment, I felt good. My arm was a lot looser, and there was less discomfort from tightness.

When I went in for a second treatment, the doctor injected the magical serum into only my hand, but he injected too much. I woke up a few days later unable to move one muscle in my hand and what little ability I had in that hand was gone. For the next month, I struggled more than I ever had and could not even tie my shoes. It made me realize how important the mobility in my left hand was, even if it was a small amount.

So as I was taking that push-up test and heard my teacher call me weak, I felt angry and defeated. I could not believe she said that when she knew about the treatment and what it had done to the strength in my arm. Although that treatment made me struggle, the strength and mobility in that arm did improve. With the help of occupational and physical therapy I became

a lot more capable.

My life as a differently abled person and a sports figure's daughter are qualities that make me stand out. I will probably always have to be aware of people's intentions for wanting to get close to me. But thanks to friends like Kirsten, I now also know I have to give people a chance to show they truly care before I decide they are not meant to be in my life.

❦

CHAPTER 9

Finding My Sport

All my life I have had a passion for sports. How could I not? It is in my blood. But for me, sports have always meant something different. It is a way of expressing my love for being able to move my body as much as I can, and a way to showcase my determination to succeed despite my disability. As a young girl, I watched my dad play football, basketball, and baseball with my brother. I wanted so badly to be part of their bond. I was amazed at how Dad threw the baseball to Wesley. The movement and fluidity of his arm as it rotated around and released the ball. As Wesley caught it, you could hear the snap of

the ball hitting the glove. I wanted that kind of ability. I wanted to be able to throw and catch a baseball, make a free throw with a basketball, and put a spiral on a football. I was not going to give up until I could.

To be an athlete, you need full use of your arms and legs. Knowing this made me want to work hard in physical and occupational therapy so I could finally play a sport. From age five to sixteen, I attempted quite a few sports, starting with swimming. My mom took me to the country club for lessons, but I soon discovered how difficult moving all four limbs at same time was for me. With the devotion of my teacher Sarah Willhalm and my own determination, I learned freestyle, breaststroke, butterfly, and backstroke. Butterfly was the hardest for me, and backstroke was my least favorite.

Unlike most children, it took me quite a few years before I felt comfortable enough to swim without floaties or a life vest. I feared the water because I felt my left arm and leg were not strong enough to keep me afloat. I feared the water... but I also loved it. Accomplishing the goal of learning to swim made

me realize I could do anything I wished, as long as I stayed determined.

Learning to swim, I not only acquired a new skill that benefitted my body in many ways, but I also gained a life-long friendship with the person who taught me. Sarah showed me the healing power of the water, how the water was not something to be afraid of but something to embrace. On land, my body is always tense, dealing with aches, pains, and firing nerves that cause the sensation of pins and needles throughout the left half of my body. In the water, my body is weightless, relaxed, and flawless—a bit of heaven on earth for me.

I'm not sure why I have cerebral palsy, but I do know I am strong enough to handle it. There was no way I was ever going to let my physical challenges stop me from doing what I loved most. I was determined to try every sport until I found one that fit. When I was five, I had a surgery that resulted in an incision on my stomach that looks like an upside-down Nike swoosh. "Just do it" is a motto I try to embrace every day, and with the complications I've faced, sometimes it's easier said than done.

My sister and I took a hip-hop dance class together when we were seven. Nicolette is a dancer, and I encourage her to never stop, because she does it so well. It's particularly amazing that she's such a great dancer because Nicolette has been deaf since she was one, and although she has cochlear implants, she is still hearing impaired. Her ability to feel the music and move so beautifully to it is a natural gift.

For me, however, dancing, especially hip-hop, was something I always struggled with. Having to move at a fast pace, with my arms and legs doing different things to upbeat music, was one of the hardest and most frustrating physical things I have ever experienced. Nevertheless, I loved dancing because it was another way I could move my body.

I danced until I was nine and then decided to move on. I still dance and have fun with friends and family, but I prefer slow dancing so that my body does not have to focus as much on what it has to do to keep up. Slow dancing only requires me to hold on to another person and sway from side to side. This is more relaxing and more personal than waving my arms

around to fast-paced music. Plus, swaying my hips is one of the easiest movements for me since my hips are one of the only parts of my body that have close to equal mobility on both side.

At age ten, I gave softball a try. Throwing a ball came naturally to me, but the process of catching the ball with a glove on my right hand and then taking the ball out of the glove and throwing it was really demanding. Softball only became a possibility when Dad introduced me to the way Jim Abbott played baseball. Jim, who played for the New York Yankees, was one of the few athletes with a disability who made it into the world of professional sports. Jim did not let the fact that he only had one hand hold him back from playing baseball. Like me, he learned to adapt so that he could play the game he loved. As a pitcher, the only way he could play was to set his glove on the stub of his right arm, throw the ball with his left, and then switch his glove so he would be ready to catch anything that came his way.

I practiced this technique every day while I played softball, but rather than set the glove on my bad

hand, I would hold it underneath my left arm. I went through the motion of throwing the ball with my glove under my left arm, and quickly changing it to my good hand to receive the ball from my teammate, over and over. When warming up, I did not have to rush to get the ball out of my glove, but in game situations, it was more difficult since I had to throw as swiftly as I could. It is hard not to make any mistakes once you have the ball because, all of a sudden, the game is in your hands.

When my coach put me at second base during a game, I fully understood the quickness needed to make outs. I felt like I was a disappointment to my team for not being quick enough. The comments and looks I got from players and coaches from different teams made me feel inadequate, and I doubted my capability as an athlete. That was something I was going to have to get used to if I wanted to play sports. Sadly, I began to lose interest in playing the game I loved to watch. As much as I loved being part of a team and being active, my dream of being a softball player faded. After quitting softball, I started to wonder if I would ever find a sport that would be a good fit for a one-handed athlete like me.

Volleyball and I had perfect chemistry. I never thought I could have so much passion for playing a sport that I would dedicate twenty hours a week to practicing my serve. Every day after school, I practiced serving over the net my dad put up on our front lawn. I served it over the net and then ran to the other side and served again. After school, I served over and over until the sun went down, and it was too dark to see the ball. Wind, rain, or shine, I was outside every single day playing volleyball. At eleven years old and 5'4", I could put topspin on my serve as consistently as anybody. Serving was something I could do with one hand and do well.

I put my heart and soul into every serve, practice, and game. But of course, I couldn't just serve over and over without expecting to be involved in the game in other ways. I learned very quickly that in any sport, you need to have more than just the ability to do one skill well. I was a great server, but I could not just rely on serving aces all the time to be guaranteed a spot in the lineup. I also had to play defense, which meant being able to dig the ball.

For a few years while playing volleyball, I tried playing with two hands. The only reason I felt the need to play with two hands was because in volleyball, the insides of both your forearms are used to pass the ball to the setter. Since I played in the back row, I had to be able to do this. Not only did I feel I had to, but I was hoping to blend in with the other players so nobody would give me any weird looks. I gave it my best effort and occasionally had some decent digs even though my left arm could not get into the correct position. As the ball would come to me, I would grab my left arm with my right and tried to angle my arms so the ball would only reflect off of my right arm. Although it was challenging and especially frustrating when I could not return the ball correctly, I put up with it because I knew my serving would make up for the skill I lacked.

After three seasons of volleyball, I decided it was time to forget about trying to blend in and do what worked best for me. I was ready to try bumping with one arm. My coaches Elbert Tsu and Willy So worked with me during every practice and before every game on perfecting the way I passed the ball. When I was outside practicing

my serve after school, I practiced my bumping as well. My favorite time to practice was when it was raining because of how muddy the grass would get. I would bump the ball in the air until I would mess up and have to dive for it so that it would not hit the ground. I loved playing as hard as I could and getting dirty, although my mom and dad had to put up with torn-up grass and mud on my clothes and the carpet. They just loved to see me enjoying something, so they let it slide.

Even though I had mastered the skill and felt more comfortable about receiving the ball if it came to me, I always felt a little unsure of myself because there was no guarantee my pass would be perfect. I used the top of my right forearm to bump the ball, so it would sometimes go in a direction I didn't want it to, because the muscles on top of my arm created an uneven surface. I could never dig the ball very well, but I dove for every ball that came my way, whether or not I thought I could make a good pass out of it.

I wasn't a consistent starter, but I was darn good at coming off the bench and making each serve count, and I was happy with my role on the team. As long

as I got a few serves in, I was satisfied. Volleyball was never about winning for me. It was about giving 100 percent to the game I loved with all of my heart. It was about overcoming my fears of being the only disabled athlete on the team. Whether I did well or not, all that mattered to me was that I tried. What I did not realize at the time was that my body could only take so much of the pressure I was putting on it.

With volleyball, I loved to test my limits. Seeing how hard I could serve the ball was always so exciting to me. With each serve, it seemed like the ball moved faster and harder, making my adrenaline pump even more. When our team was on defense and I would play the back row, I would dive for any ball near me that came close to hitting the ground. If I did not come home with any new bumps and bruises, it meant I did not work hard enough in practice.

It was during my freshman year that I discovered a different perspective on the level of intensity I put into playing volleyball. I had thought giving it my all physically was the only way I deserved to play. I did not want to take any of my ability for granted, but before

long, it got to be too much. Ninth grade was the first year I suffered any real injuries. When you think about it, a physical disability is like having an injury that never goes away, and I was adding to it by not listening to my body.

I pushed myself way too hard that first year. During practices, I did sprints with the team. My left hip developed tendonitis, which took a year of physical therapy and anti-inflammatories to heal. It still flares up every now and then because I continue to be active, but nothing like I experienced that year. Because of all the running I did, I have a painful bunion on my left foot. From serving so much, I developed back spasms that required physical therapy, although I did not mind because there is nothing like a good back massage.

I did feel a little guilty because this added pain meant more treatment my parents had to pay for, but I know they wanted me to continue to enjoy life by doing what I loved. I knew I could have avoided the added stress on my body, but I was willing to do anything to keep playing. I even hid a few injuries from my coaches—that's how badly I wanted to play. The

pain in my left foot and ankle got to the point where I knew if I kept playing and putting that kind of impact on my body, I would not have such a promising future physically. There were nights when I would come home, get into the shower, and just cry because of the pain I was in, but the emotional pain of the decision I had to make was even greater.

As I stood in the shower with my aching feet on the hard, wet ground and the hot, steamy water hitting my shoulders, I looked down at what had already seemed so crippled. I then pictured my future self, unable to walk normally, run around, and move my body. How was I going to play with my children if I could not do those things anymore? It would not be fair to them, my future husband, or anyone in my life to have to worry about me more than they should.

I realized that how I treat my body in the present affects my body in the future. I was devoted to volley-ball for eight full years and had no choice but to quit. I learned the hard way the importance of listening to my body. Soon after making my final decision, I told

my family and friends and then my coaches. Quitting volleyball was the hardest decision I ever made. Not because I was pressured to be an athlete like everyone else in my family, but because I felt so deeply for it. Everyone in my life could see that. I did not understand how much volleyball meant to me until I did not have it anymore.

ABOVE: Dave and Kandice Righetti

BELOW: Sisters: Kayla and Kandice

ABOVE: Triplets: Nicolette, Wesley, and Natalee

RIGHT: Natalee on her first birthday

BELOW: Natalee at the ballpark

ABOVE: Nicolette, Wesley, and Natalee at age 7
BELOW: Nicolette, Wesley, and Natalee at age 19

ABOVE: Natalee playing volleyball in high school

BELOW: The Righetti family after the San Francisco Giants won the 2010 World Series

CHAPTER 10

Life Lessons

I thought I was destined to be one of the few professional athletes with a disability. Yet as I lay in bed, I wondered why I had the ability to play sports if they were only going to put me through all this pain. I spent nights crying myself to sleep. Never before had I asked "Why me? Why was I the one to get a physically debilitating condition that would hinder me forever?" until it threatened to take volleyball from me. I spent what felt like forever trying to figure out how something I loved so much could put me through so much physical pain and force me to cut it out of my life.

Volleyball meant the world to me and was the one thing in my life that I could give my whole heart to and not worry about it winding up broken. Or so I thought. I came to understand that anything worth giving your heart to has the potential to hurt you. That is a risk we take all the time, sometimes without even realizing it. Falling for someone who doesn't feel the same and living with physical ailments and fading friendships are all ways I have learned your heart can be broken. Life puts us in situations we never thought possible, and when they happen, our emotions can get the best of us.

After making the decision to not play volleyball competitively anymore, it took me a long time to feel happy again. I had become so angry. Angry because I felt like I let my disability get in the way of my dream of playing sports. For the rest of my freshman year and my sophomore year, I battled a lot of anxiety, which made the burden of my physical challenge even worse.

I didn't let anyone know what I was going through at the time, and even had a panic attack during one of my classes without telling anyone. With my stomach weak and in knots, my heart raced faster than

I have ever felt before. While other students sat in their seats listening to the teacher, I felt trapped like I had no place to go. Something had taken control of my body. Taking deep breaths, I told the feeling over and over to go away. Maybe I should have told someone what was happening, but I was too stubborn. I knew it was only anxiousness due to stress, and I was not going to let it take control of my life. Not having volleyball as a stress release brought on a lot of different feelings. I became unsure of myself and confused about my place in the world.

Volleyball had been my safe haven when other things in my life were not going well, and now that was gone. Thankfully, I had my family to lean on for support, and friends who allowed me to feel vulnerable during my weakest moments. There is nothing more meaningful than a healing friendship, one based on support and encouragement through difficult times. Those are the people I always come back to because I feel stronger every time I talk with them. Without support from loved ones, dealing with something like a disability and all the challenges it comes with can feel impossible

to face. At that time in my life when I was trying to accept giving up volleyball, support from friends had a big impact on my ability to accept the way things were going in my life.

Volleyball was not out of my life completely. During sophomore year, my volleyball coach, who understood the passion I had for the sport, asked me to be a player/coach. Although I did not play in games, I had the opportunity to see volleyball from a coach's perspective. I helped with drills during practice, gave signs to the girls during games, and sat on the bench while I cheered for my team. The gym was my sanctuary, and as long as I was involved in volleyball somehow, I was happy.

I got a great surprise at the end of the practice before the championship game. The girls and coaches asked me to play in the last game! I was speechless. Tears welled up in my eyes as I smiled the biggest smile. I immediately accepted their offer and went home to tell my family and friends the exciting news.

As I stepped into the gym in kneepads and my

uniform, the familiar feeling of pre-game nerves hit me. I loved the way volleyball made me feel. The physical energy creating excitement and every swing of my arm making me feel powerful. Every time I held that ball in my hand before I tossed it up in the air, I was in control. The game was in my hands, and it was up to me to serve as many aces as I could.

After warming up with the team, I felt pretty confident about my ability to get the ball over the net, but I was nervous I would choke in front of my family, friends, and team since I had not been in a game for a year. Once the game started, all I could focus on was when it would be my turn to sub in and serve for my teammate.

As I stepped behind the serving line, everything seemed to be in hyper-speed. Adrenaline rushed through my veins as I went into my zone. I tossed the ball up and felt like it was rising in slow motion. When the ball hit its peak, I quickly swung my arm around and snapped my wrist forward with great force as my palm met the ball. The ball sailed over the net. I did it! Then I got two more over after my team rallied for

points. After all that time had passed, I got to serve in a game and did better than I expected. We were league champions, and it was the best day of the season by far.

I was on cloud nine that night. In fact, my body could not settle down even after I went to bed. I had enough energy to serve a hundred more balls. I will never forget that last game, because my coaches and team had given me the opportunity of a lifetime: the opportunity to feel like me again. Even though that was the last game I played competitively, I continued to play for fun for another year, until I realized all the wear and tear on my arm was doing more harm than good.

Once I developed tendonitis in my right arm, I decided it was enough. I didn't pick up a volleyball—or any ball—for a very long time. Leaving volleyball was difficult, but it was the right thing for me. My right arm is all I have, and if I choose sports over good health, I am looking at a tough road ahead. However, physical activity is still part of my life.

The health of my body is very important to me

and the better shape I stay in, the better my body feels. To stay in good physical condition, cardio and other exercises are part of my daily routine. Walking on the treadmill or riding on a stationary bike not only builds my muscular endurance, but it also helps balance out my unsteady gait.

I recently took an indoor spin-cycling class and fell in love with it. That class put me in the best shape I have ever been in. My left leg feels stronger, and I have the strength to last a whole day on my feet. My left leg feels almost as strong as my right leg now. The toughest thing about exercising on cardio machines is focusing on my left leg, so that it keeps the same pace as my right leg. A lot of times I move my right leg slower than my left, so that my left leg has to do most of the work. The competitor in me sometimes gets frustrated working at a slower pace on a bike or treadmill, because I know I have the energy to go faster, but I enjoy always trying to improve.

The best part of my morning workouts is the hour-long adrenaline rush. I have the energy and stamina that makes me feel I could keep going and

never stop. I treat workouts the way I treat life—I keep moving forward with the intention of never giving up on myself before I reach my goal. The most important thing when working to be the healthiest you can be is the mentality you have. In my mind, when I am working out, I am training for a marathon, the marathon of life.

CHAPTER 11

New Beginnings

After graduation, I planned to attend the University of San Francisco with one of my closest friends. I had visited the campus a couple of times and thought the atmosphere was beautiful. Before I made any final decisions, my parents warned me that the campus was very hilly and questioned whether it would be too much for my body to handle. But my heart was already committed to that school and sharing a room with Olivia Palaad. All I was focused on that summer was getting prepared for being away from home.

The spring before my first year of college, I was going through a lot of personal issues. I had parted ways with a person who I cared a lot about, and it affected me deeply. All I wanted to do was get away and focus on the next part of my life. I was ready and fully capable of being on my own, but I didn't realize how overwhelming college would be.

My parents were right. The campus was too much for my body to handle. After just five days at USF, my body did not feel as strong or energized as it normally does. During orientation, I looked around the gym at all the students. They seemed so awake and alert. Was I the only one who felt so wiped out? Following a full day of walking around campus, I was too tired to do anything else. I did not even have the energy to get daily exercise, which is very important to me since it has always been my way of reducing stress.

I am not like the average college student when it comes to staying up late and sleeping in. By evening, my body has had enough of being out and about so in a way, I am sort of a homebody. I have never been able

to sleep in either. Ever since I was little, I would be up at 6 a.m. no matter what time I went to bed the night before. My body works like a clock. It knows when it is time for bed and when it is time to wake up. I didn't realize until I went to USF how regimented my daily routine is, and how crucial it is for me to stick to that routine. Although I should have expected the dorms to be noisy, especially at night, as a light sleeper I had the hardest time falling asleep. I'm in bed by 10 or 10:30 p.m. almost every night, and it only took five days of being at that school for me to realize I was not doing the right thing for myself. By the fifth day, I was ready to go home and enroll at a junior college.

I knew it was important to listen to my body so my mom quickly helped me move out of my dorm. It became clear I wouldn't be able to thrive at the University of San Francisco and I didn't want to waste any more time or money, so I got out of there as fast as I could. The hardest part about leaving was that it felt like I was walking away from my friend, like I had broken a pact and a promise to be there with her through it all. We had always talked about how we would be

there for each other through college and when we got married and had children.

I felt even worse once I was home and going to nearby Foothill College. Even though I was getting just as good of an education, I was lonely and knew my friend and former roommate was probably even lonelier. I was worried that my friendship with my dearest friend from high school would fade.

I now understand that although some people in my life that I hold closest to my heart do not live near me, it doesn't mean we can't have a strong friendship. They are kind of like angels. You cannot always see them but you know they are there in spirit, and that makes them special. Absence really does make the heart grow fonder. If there is one thing I have learned from having a family member who travels a lot and friends I only get to see every once in a while, it is how to love from a distance and keep those relationships strong.

There are people in life who come and go but these people—true friends and family—make it easy to be loyal. They are the people who allow you to learn

and grow with each conversation, who touch your soul and who make you want to open your heart. To them, I do not hesitate to give my heart.

At times I've been hurt, not understanding why certain things in my life didn't go the way I hoped they would. I've faced physical struggles that I had to acknowledge every day, given my whole heart to a game that taught me way more than how to serve a volleyball, and fallen for someone I knew would never fall for me. I realize life is full of heartbreaks, but I also realize I cannot live in fear. What kind of person would I be if I kept my heart to myself because I feared getting hurt?

Life wouldn't be so greatly desired if it were not filled with emotional ups and downs. I say what I feel, do what I feel, and believe in what I feel even if it means putting my emotions at risk. I know I have been blessed with people who really care about me, when my words and actions of kindness are reciprocated with just as much or even more love. From the life I have lived so far and the people I have met, I am strong enough to separate those who are true to me from the people who are not. I know in my heart that the people who

are in my life right now, and hopefully those I am destined to meet, will support me as I support them— especially those who have been there for me through difficult times in my life.

From everything that I have gone through, I now understand that life is ever changing and that life will forever change you. As long as you stay true to your heart and let life guide you, you will find your purpose, as I believe I have finally found mine.

Purpose

Live with purpose, and your

life will never lose meaning.

CHAPTER 12

Nicolette and Wesley

From everything I've been through, I know we all have a purpose for being here and a reason for being given both our obstacles and our gifts. Although my physical challenges were more severe than my sister Nicolette's and brother Wesley's, they also had long-term effects from our early arrival into this world.

Because of the medication she needed at birth, my parents discovered that Nicolette had become deaf by the age of one. She was born with the ability to hear, and had it taken away from her just like that. Mom and Dad did not waste time getting Nicolette hearing aids and speech therapy. At four years old, she got cochlear implants and with them, she has regained about 80 percent of her hearing.

The Jean Weingarten Peninsula Oral School for the Deaf (JWPOSD) in Redwood City, California, where my sister learned to listen and talk, was a blessing not just for Nicolette, but for our entire family. She was surrounded by other hearing-impaired kids, which helped Niki feel completely normal.

When we were five, Wesley and I joined Nicolette at JWPOSD. As one of the few hearing students there, I not only learned how to help my sister or other students when they did not understand something, but I also got to experience what it felt like to be an outsider. At the time, I had no idea being in that kind of environment was going to prepare me for many more moments where I would feel like an outcast.

That school was a safe place for Nicolette, where she did not have to worry about what people thought of her cochlear implants or the way she talked. However, what JWPOSD really did for my sister was prepare her for the hearing world. When she was nine, she was fully mainstreamed. I loved it because she could finally be at the same school as my brother and me. But being where the class curriculum is not designed for the hearing impaired proved to be challenging for Nicolette. She did not let that stop her though. With the help of an aide, she whizzed through high school.

One thing that Niki's school for the deaf brought out in her was her natural talent for dance. My sister is fearless. Although she was always the only hearing-impaired girl in the class, she danced as hard as and even better than anyone else. That is what I have always thought anyway. You will not see many hearing-impaired people in a dance class or performing on stage.

That is why Nicolette is so amazing. Although she cannot hear the words of the music she dances to, she feels it and dances with all of her heart. With each move she makes, you feel the passion she has for dance. Oh, how I wish I could move like her! I love watching her dance, and with each of her performances, I get the chills or a little teary-eyed because she has come so far

since being in that incubator as a newborn. Dance is her gift, and I know she will never stop loving it.

Out of the three of us, my brother suffered the least damage from birth, and it wasn't until he was in school that my parents realized there were some difficulties to address. In preschool and kindergarten, Wesley and I were in the same classes. My brother was a very hyper kid and would always be singing and humming in class. Although it may have kept him from focusing, Wesley's upbeat personality never failed to make everyone smile.

From age four to sixteen, playing baseball was the perfect way for him to release his energy. I loved going to his games and watching him because again, he never failed to entertain everyone. During games where he was in the outfield, Wesley made plays by diving for the ball with the ending motion of rolling to his feet. There were times when he got so caught up in entertaining himself that we would catch him doing cartwheels in the outfield. My brother continued to struggle with the ability to focus, which made school tough to get through.

During his sophomore year, Wesley decided that baseball was not number one in his heart anymore. I am sure quitting baseball was not an easy decision for my brother, since our dad was a professional ball player, but no one in my family, especially my dad, ever pressured him.

Despite our support and my dad's reassurance, I think quitting baseball was hard for Wes. Having a professional athlete for a father automatically puts pressure on a son who plays the same sport. Teammates expected him to be a star athlete and dominant pitcher just like his dad. It is hard to enjoy doing something when the pressure becomes too much to handle, but no matter what Wesley chooses to do, pressure will come with it. As human beings, we naturally put pressure on ourselves to do well at the things we want to be successful at.

We should have taken Wesley's love for singing when he was young as a sign of things to come. Once Wes stopped playing baseball, he was able to enjoy what he really loved doing—singing and playing guitar. His voice, strong and pure, always puts me at ease. I could

listen to him sing for hours. You can't get a voice like his just by practicing and learning the notes. He is meant to sing.

Wesley plays guitar by ear and sings based on the tune he hears when he plays. I am amazed at how gifted he is. At times, I may push him harder than he wishes I would, but it is only because, as someone who deals with physical challenges every day, I know how amazing it feels to accomplish something you work hard for. I believe he is capable of doing great things. I hope he never stops and musters up the courage one day to show the world what is in his heart through music, because he was given a musical soul for a reason. With the will to make his voice heard, he could bring joy to many people. I just know it.

CHAPTER 13

Sibling Support

I was a total tomboy when I was young. My mom says I was too cute to pull off the look but I was still one at heart. I went through a phase of wanting to wear my brother's clothes and hats all the time. I felt if I were one of the boys, it would bring me closer to my brother. As it turns out I didn't need to act like a boy to relate to Wesley. As brother and sister, we loved being around each other.

Being an early riser, I would wake Wesley up in the morning so we could play with his toy dinosaurs. We would also spend mornings watching *Tom and*

Jerry and other cartoons together. In preschool, Wesley would push me on the swing every day at lunchtime and give me a ride on the two-seated tricycle. We had some very good times together as kids, and even though we are quite different from each other now, we still find things to talk about.

While I loved being a tough tomboy, I also loved being a girl. Nicolette and I spent hours on the weekends playing with Barbies and dressing up in Mom's old clothes. The weekend seemed to go on forever, and we loved every minute of it. We would make up stories for each Barbie character. Ken and Barbie were always in love with each other, but then something drastic would happen, making them end their relationship. The break-up was short lived, for Barbie and Ken always found their way back to each other.

During dress up, we would wear Mom's dresses and high heels with confidence, acting like we were grown women with husbands and children. My sister and I still like to imagine our futures and come up with scenarios for how our lives will turn out. Our connection goes deeper than that though. We are each other's sidekicks and always have been. Whenever I've needed help doing something, she is right there. She knows me so well that most of the time I don't even need to ask for help. When we are with a group of people and Nicolette is having a hard time understanding what is being said, I am there to clarify anything she is confused about. We know one day a husband will take the place of our role in helping each other as much as we do, but until then, we remain each other's strength whenever we need it.

As a little girl, I would watch my brother and sister play together in our pool every summer as I sat on the steps, wishing I had the ability to swim like they did. I remember them learning to ride a bike and rollerblade and becoming very good at both. Although I tried to accomplish riding a bike, my body was too unbalanced to stay up for long. A lot of times I felt like an outsider looking in, as Wesley and Nicolette enjoyed fun times together, but I made up for not being involved in certain activities by creating a special relationship with each of them.

Nicolette, Wesley, and I have a bond that can

never be broken. We have watched each other struggle, succeed, and fail, but we never lose faith in one another. I get so much joy out of watching them carry out their abilities the best they can, and I hope they continue, because just surviving when they were born shows they can overcome when the odds are against them. Seeing the way they live their lives is what motivates me. They are the strength behind ever step I take, every challenge I attack, and every goal I strive for.

CHAPTER 14

Helping Others

I am only mildly affected with cerebral palsy. Sometimes I can't help but feel a little guilty when I think of how many people are severely affected with this disability and have to use a wheelchair. The aches, pains, and obstacles I go through every day are probably ten times worse for someone who has severe cerebral palsy.

Throughout my toddler and teen years, I witnessed firsthand the different levels of severity that someone with cerebral palsy can have. Every week, as I walked through the gym for physical and occupational therapy, I saw the other kids who were in wheelchairs

and on crutches. It became clear how well off I was compared to others. During my physical therapy sessions, I would hear screams and cries coming from different areas of the room. Although with each stretch and pull of my arm and leg came immense pain, the sounds of the other children's pain is what I really felt.

As I got older, I began to realize how much ability I had and I felt so blessed. I had the freedom to run around, play sports, swim, and learn to drive. But as each year passed, walking through that gym for physical therapy gave me this feeling of selfishness. I have a disability too and deserved to get the best help I could, but as I heard those screams and cries of pain, I questioned why I got so lucky and they did not. I wished for them to have my ability, and the experience of running on their own two feet. I wanted to be able to give something in return and help them experience what I have.

Most people do not know what kind of career they want until they go to college and have the chance to explore their options. Since eighth grade, I've thought about one day working for the Giants in the public relations department. I figured since baseball has a special place in my heart and I enjoy working with people, that would be the perfect fit. However, during one of my physical therapy sessions, I discovered my ability to inspire others just like me. I got the opportunity to meet a little girl who was also going to physical and occupational therapy. At the time, she was about nine and I was fifteen. As I faced her while we were talking, I felt as though I was looking in a mirror at a younger me. A spunky little girl with glasses, she did not let the fact that CP affected her right side keep her from trying things like sports.

I told her about all the sports I had played and that it was worthwhile despite the ups and downs. I made it my purpose that day to inspire her with a positive outlook on her disability, but what she did for me was even greater. At nine years old, she probably didn't understand how remarkable it was for her to strive to do everything people with two good hands can do. After we spoke and she heard from someone older yet so similar to her, I think she started to see that her ability could allow her to do anything she desired. From then on, my goal was to be the best role model I could be, for people young and old.

All my life, I have felt so fortunate to have the amount of physical ability that I have. Through the years of struggles and success, I have learned to see the ability I was given in a positive light. I cannot speak for others with disabilities, but I see my physical challenge as a gift. Because only one side of my body is disabled, I am able to understand what it feels like to have normal mobility in my arms and legs, but also what it's like to not have enough mobility. This allows me to relate to all kinds of people, ranging from the very disabled to those who are not disabled at all.

I grew up around adults because of my dad's career, so talking to people of all ages comes naturally to me and I've had plenty of opportunities to talk to others about my challenges and positive outlook on life. Last year, I was honored to participate in a panel for Fathers' and Daughters' Day at Giants stadium with other Bay Area sports figures and their daughters. My dad, Nicolette, and I were there, as well as Mike

Krukow and his daughter Tessa, Duane Kuiper and his daughter, Dannon, and Brent Jones and his daughter Courtney. The pictures from that day show me smiling and laughing and definitely reflect how comfortable I was talking to the crowd. Having these types of experiences prepared me for what I am meant to do and hope to do for a long time. But it wasn't until an event at my high school last year that I realized what exactly that was.

In the spring of 2010, I organized a Disability Awareness Day at Mountain View High School in Los Altos, California, where students participated in events like writing with their nondominant hand and singing while blindfolded, to get a sense of what it is like to have a disability. It felt great to provide a way for high school students to learn about those who are different from them, and hopefully become more compassionate in the process. It was also nice to help others with differences know they are an important part of the community. I also formed a high school club called Sky's the Limit, where students can talk about issues and support each other. Seeing some of my ideas in

action made it clear that what I want to do is motivate others with disabilities and also help people relate to those with disabilities better.

I was given enough of a disability to be able to empathize with others who struggle physically, and I would not want my life to be any other way. I love my body, how it challenges me and what it has taught me about life. Without it, I wouldn't be as determined, strong, or self-disciplined as I am. It has grounded me and prepared me for anything I wish to do in life. Now my purpose in life is to inspire others to pursue their dreams, no matter what obstacles they face.

I have learned to keep reaching for my goals whether or not I think I can reach them. It is important, no matter how scared or unsure you are about where your life is going, that you give it all you have and at least try. You never know what opportunities could arise. They could lead to good things happening that you never imagined.

Having cerebral palsy has taught me to make up for the lack of feeling I have on my left side by feeling with all of my heart. Because of my disability, I have come to appreciate each moment of every day, even though sometimes I might let situations get the best of me. During those rare moments when I'm feeling down and frustrated about my physical condition, I remind myself of what I have struggled through, how far I have come, and how fortunate I am for the ability I do have.

We all have hardships we have to deal with, whether it's a disability of some sort, a life-threatening disease, or having to watch a loved one go through a bout of misfortune. All you can do is fight through it and try to look at the life you have been given from a more positive perspective. Every challenge I face is a learning experience, and I won't let my challenges keep me from living a happy life. That is the message I hope to get across to anyone I come in contact with.

I now have my sights set on a career where I get the opportunity to motivate people with disabilities through sharing my life story. I enjoy encouraging others who may struggle with a disability, whether it is physical or mental. I would like to help as many

people as I can by showing them that it is possible to live your life the way you want, despite the obstacles you face. Life isn't a breeze, but it is the attitude you choose to live with that makes overcoming those obstacles worth it.

I hope my story will inspire others to live their lives to the best of their ability, whatever that may be. I hope to inspire others for the rest of my life. I would like to make a living by speaking about the adversity I've overcome and how it has made me a better person. I will continue to fight through life in the hopes that others will see my efforts and want to live their lives with the same kind of intensity that I have. Maybe one day, I will find someone who believes in my story and will want to be the person who motivates me to keep going, someone who will fuel my fire.

Destiny

Do not let fears of not

knowing what may lie

ahead keep you from

fulfilling your dreams.

CHAPTER 15

A Love Story Not Yet Written

When I lie in bed at night, I reflect on my accomplishments and the struggles I have faced. I think about my hopes and dreams of one day finding someone who will want to tackle the challenges of life with me. Then I pray. I know if I go through life without a companion, I will be fine. I have proven to myself that I am capable of almost everything I attempt to do. But still... I hope to find that special someone and together create a strong partnership. That someone will help me when I am being too proud to admit I need help. That someone will allow me to feel vulnerable and hurt when I am tired of being tough enough to handle everything my body goes through on a daily basis.

What I've learned from watching my parents and the circumstances they've faced is that in every marriage, a strong bond and sense of teamwork is crucial to keep a relationship going. When both people are being supported by one another while going through challenges, whether they are medical, financial, or occupational, things become a little easier. To me, the way you show people you love them is by supporting them through their successes and their failures.

That is what I hope someone will do for me and what I know I will do for him. What many people may not realize is being with someone with a disability does not have to get in the way of a relationship. In a sense, it is a way to feel more connected to each other. My disability is my secret weapon. Someday it may also be one of the best secrets to my lasting marriage.

When I was younger and thought about my future, I felt like I would end up being a burden to the man I married because of all the things he would have to help me with. "So why get married and put someone through that?" I thought. I realize now that helping take care of me will help make him become more of a man. A man to me is not defined by his physical strength, ruggedness, or height, although having someone with those qualities would not be such a bad thing. A real man has inner strength, is devoted and self-assured, knows right from wrong, and is confident yet humble.

The right guy for me will be able to react to the challenges that arise. This means that he will have a strong sense of who he is and what he is capable of. The right guy will not view me as burden, because he will understand that helping each other is what marriage is all about. He may have to help me physically a little more than a nondisabled wife, but that will help make us a unique duo and a strong team, and create a lasting partnership.

One day I will finally have my right-hand man— or, in my case, left-hand man. I will look for a man who has faced adversity in his life and is not afraid of a challenge. Although I am forced to look toward a future of continued physical challenges, I am not afraid of all the mountains, for I know he will be climbing them with me. There will be a lot of laughs in our future, but I'm sure a lot of tears as well. After all, life would not be as interesting or exciting if it was perfect.

Among my many hopes and dreams is to be a mom. My mom did not let the obstacle of infertility stop her from finding love or conceiving children with my dad. Because of her determination, my brother, sister, and I get to experience the world. When my time comes to have children, I may find myself in my mom's position and possibly not be able to carry my own children. It may be too risky for me and my baby, because of the physical stress it would cause, but also because of my epilespy medication, which could posibly cause birth defects. Down the road, I will be open to having children any way I can, and my mom will be the first person I go to for advice.

If it were not for my mom, I cannot say that having children would be one of my life-long dreams. Having the responsibility of being a mom is tough enough, let alone being a mom of triplets. I watch her do what she does and am amazed and inspired by her. Since I was a little girl, I have watched my mom. Back then it was watching her put on makeup and get dressed up to go out to dinner with my dad on those rare occasions when he had some time off. I would look at my mom, wishing I would end up looking as beautiful as her.

I still watch her but with a different perspective now. I study her as if I am getting ready to be a mother. I understand that I am young and have a few years to go before I begin that phase in my life. Until then, I know that being a mother is one of my purposes in life. To be a mom, you have to be many things: a teacher, a motivational speaker, and a caregiver. These are all things I have become since learning to cope with the struggles of living with cerebral palsy.

Being a parent will not only make me stronger, but will make my marriage stronger. Our team of two will grow into a family bond as tight as my family's bond has grown to be. I am not worried about my children looking at me differently because, to them, the way I complete daily tasks will be normal. As my children grow, things may get a little more challenging. My family will not always be available to help me. I may find it difficult to do things like style my daughter's hair or help my son get dressed. Hopefully, these situations will make my children stronger and more self-sufficient human beings. There will be times when they have no choice but to do things for themselves. I have learned to get through life and sharing my experiences will prepare them for the many curveballs life will throw their way.

I pray that one day I will have the privilege of going through life with the right partner beside me. I do not know when that will be or who it will be, but all the same, I know it will happen. As for becoming a mother, however it happens, I know it is in my future. I have been given a gift, not a burden. My disability has prepared me for the challenges ahead, as well as the ability to fulfill my dreams. I am eager to find out what the years will bring, but like everyone else, I will have to wait and see what my future holds. I have always wanted to write a love story. Maybe one day, I will get to write my own.

ACKNOWDGEMENTS

Many thanks to my family for their constant support: my
parents Kandice and Dave Righetti, my sister Nicolette
and brother Wesley, my Righetti and Owen grandparents,
aunt Kayla Campbell and her family, and all my aunts,
uncles, and cousins.

I also want to thank my friends Sarah Willhalm, Olivia
Palaad, Kirsten Wessbecher, and Christiana Harvey; the
Frandsen family; and my volleyball coaches Elbert Tsu
and Willy So.

Thanks to Pam Baer for believing in my book and
connecting me with Julie Thompson, who organized
my manuscript and consulted on this project. Thanks
also to Cathleen O'Brien for design and Jennifer Block
Martin for copyediting, all of which helped transform
my stories into a book that tells my story.

Natalee Righetti has never let her disability
stop her and knows that in many ways, it
has made her much stronger. She organized
a Disability Awareness Day while in high
school—now an annual event. Natalee is a
college student and motivational speaker.

Read more on Natalee's blog,
nataleerighetti.blogspot.com.